WHAT'S WORTH

FIGHTING FOR IN

HEADSHIP?

WHAT'S WORTH

FIGHTING FOR IN

HEADSHIP?

Strategies for taking charge of the headship

MICHAEL FULLAN

OPEN UNIVERSITY PRESS
in association with the
Ontario Public School Teachers' Federation

First published 1988 by the Ontario Public School Teachers'
Federation
This edition published 1992 by Open University Press in
association with the OPSTF

Open University Press
Celtic Court
22 Ballmoor
Buckingham
MK18 1XW

First Published 1992

A catalogue record of this book is available from the British
Library

ISBN 0–335–15754–8

Typeset by Type Study, Scarborough
Printed in Great Britain by
J. W. Arrowsmith Limited, Bristol

CONTENTS

PREFACE TO THE

BRITISH EDITION

The head is in the midst of ever increasing demands, overload and imposition on schools by political forces at all levels of society. This book examines and proposes to heads, what's worth fighting for, under conditions of enormous challenges.

Although the book has its origins in the context of Canadian schools, I believe that the most basic problems are similar in the United Kingdom, as are the guidelines for action recommended in this book. Overload, dependency, isolation, arbitrary political shifts, imposed and alienating policies, and the inability of heads to control events and to empower themselves and their teachers to transcend and transform these difficulties are common across national boundaries.

Yet, key aspects of the UK context *are* different and do matter. England and Wales have their new National Curriculum, operating as an oppressive constraint or constructive opportunity, depending on one's viewpoint and response. The Education Reform Act of 1988, pushing the Local Management of Schools (LMS), has given school governors additional powers, and has weakened the role of Local Education Authorities to the point that they may disappear or become the least important partner in the educational enterprise.

The culture and ethos of school leadership also differ in fundamental ways across nations. For example, North American heads have perhaps depended too much on external administrative regulations, and not exercised enough discretion and initiative over curriculum and teaching in their schools. The United Kingdom, on the other hand, has offered many examples of independent heads who 'run their schools' autonomously often with a strong focus on curriculum and teaching. But perhaps this high degree of individualistic autonomy has made heads and schools politically vulnerable when imposition does occur.

With or without a National Curriculum and testing apparatus, the freedom of the head has more often been the freedom of the individual head than of the group or school. Improvement, this book argues, is the collective responsibility of the school. This is imperative. And neither published guidelines nor individual autonomy will make it happen. What's worth fighting for in schools, therefore, is 'interactive professionalism' where heads and teachers work together, become less autonomous and isolated, more open and risk taking, better skilled through continuous development, and ultimately more empowered in accomplishing what they set out to do.

Almost everywhere, headteachers are overloaded and undervalued. Governments and systems should treat their school heads better, but usually they do not. History suggests that those outside the school are unlikely to make the first move to improve the lot of heads. Heads working with teachers will need to take more of the initiative themselves, not just in holding off unreasonable demands, nor even in bargaining for better conditions (though these things are important), but also in making constructive improvements of their own, as a professional community. Some of the research we cite suggests that examples of such constructive practice already exist. But they need to be broadened, strengthened and developed. This book (and its companion volume, *What's Worth Fighting For in Your School?*, Fullan and Hargreaves, 1992) are meant to stimulate such improvements among teachers and heads as professional communities.

FOREWORD

The role of the school head has never been perceived to be an easy one. Today it is continually becoming more diverse and complex as the needs and demands of our society change. How does the school head determine priorities, develop strategies, implement programmes and assess growth? How can the primary school head take charge? Why does Fullan challenge school administrators to 'err on the side of autonomy'? This study, in realistic terms, describes the world of the headship. The author reflects on the demands of this role in the context of what he describes as a nonrational world. He articulates a new concept of the headship and delineates clearly what is worth fighting for in this role.

This book is a challenge issued to educators in, or aspiring to, positions of added responsibility. Michael Fullan's view of the school head's role will elicit debate. His recommendations regarding head autonomy will represent an opportunity for innovation. For those interested in the role of the head, this volume will raise questions, discussion and reflection. It may also become a catalyst for action. Different people will respond to the challenge in different ways. Michael Fullan recommends a very definite and individual approach.

This publication is in keeping with the Ontario Public School Teachers' Federation's long tradition of highlighting a broad range of effective alternatives in all aspects of the head's leadership role. The recommendations and conclusions are those of the author and do not necessarily represent the OPSTF policy or position on the role of the headship. The Ontario Public School Teachers' Federation expresses gratitude and appreciation to Michael Fullan for his contribution to our profession.

David Kendall
President, OPSTF

ACKNOWLEDGEMENTS

I would like to thank the Ontario Public School Teachers' Federation for initiating this commissioned study. Responsibility for monitoring the work rested with the members of the OPSTF Positions of Added Responsibility committee. My sincere thanks to OPSTF secretariat members Noel Clark and Linda Grant for their assistance in producing the monograph. John Boich, Bruce Joyce, Ken Leithwood, Matt Miles, Paul Shaw and Dennis Thiessen made very helpful comments on the first draft.

THE AUTHOR

Michael Fullan is Dean of the Faculty of Education, University of Toronto, and Professor in Sociology of Education. Prior to this appointment he was an Assistant Director (Academic) at The Ontario Institute for Studies in Education. An innovator and leader in teacher education, he has, since joining the University of Toronto: organized a learning consortium of four school boards and two teacher education institutions; through The Learning Consortium sponsored three Summer Institutes for cooperative learning and coaching; and for the University of Toronto, in cooperation with OISE, founded a Joint Centre for Teacher Development. As well as these joint projects, he participates as researcher, consultant, trainer, and policy adviser on a wide range of educational change projects with school systems, teachers' federations, research and development institutes, and government agencies in Canada and internationally. In June 1990, as the first recipient of the Canadian Association of Teacher Educators (CATE) Award

of Excellence, he was recognized for 'outstanding contribution to his profession and to teacher education' and was
seen as a 'researcher/scholar/practitioner of the highest
calibre' by that organization.

He has published widely on the topic of educational
change and reform. His most recent publications are (with
S. Stiegelbauer), *The New Meaning of Educational Change*
(1991) and *Successful School Improvement* (1992).

INTRODUCTION

Overload fosters dependency.

This is not a research study; it is a thoughtpiece and guide for action for school heads. The premise is that the 'system', however unwittingly, fosters dependency on the part of heads. Sometimes the pressure for dependency comes from below, as in teacher expectations; sometimes it comes from above, as in government directives. Paradoxically, dependency is fostered both by emphasis on tradition and by demands for innovation. The role of heads in implementing innovations is more often than not a case of being on the receiving end of externally initiated changes. Dependency is created through the constant bombardment of new tasks and continual interruptions on the job which keep heads occupied or at least off balance.

Overload fosters dependency. Heads are either overloaded with what they are doing or overloaded with all the things they think they should be doing. Dependency, I will argue, may also be internalized or too easily tolerated by heads themselves.

By dependency I mean that one's actions are predominantly shaped, however unintentionally, by events and/or by actions or directions of others. Empowerment, taking charge, and otherwise playing a central role in determining what is done is the opposite of dependency. Taking charge does not mean that one eschews interdependencies. As will become clear, effective empowerment and interdependency go hand in hand.

While this book makes the case that heads must take charge of their own destiny, it explicitly rejects any notion of isolated autonomy. Indeed, the empowered, interdependent head has and experiences great social responsibilities to act. Empowerment and accountability, far from being polar opposites, are intimately related. The empowered head working collaboratively is far more responsible than the dependent head. Dependency is closer to helplessness than it is to responsiveness. The message here is that individual heads, with or without help, must transcend the problem of dependency if it is to be resolved, and hence, if heads are to be effective.

The study will examine the problem of dependency and how to overcome it. Chapter 1 starts with a description of how bad things are. I call this situation the 'nonrational' world of the head, borrowing a term from Patterson *et al.* (1986). The purpose of this choice is to indicate what heads are facing, but it also, however, is meant to reflect a glimmer of hope, since the system is not downright irrational. The term also anticipates that the answer lies not in wishing for more reasonable and rational circumstances, since 'if only' statements are not very productive starting points for solving problems. In addition to characterizing the existing system as unreasonable, Chapter 1 also contains the charge that to a certain extent the problem is 'within'; that is, many heads are limiting themselves as to what positive steps they can take. The chapter ends with a discussion of the role of the head and of the change which indicates that, along with potential, there are dangerous tendencies in current practices. These practices tend to reinforce dependency, albeit ironically in the service of innovation.

In Chapter 2 the point of departure is that the present system simply is not working. Despite great effort and considerable attention paid to the headship, there is little evidence that we are making substantial gains. The yield for the effort seems much too small to warrant following existing paths. I will not argue that I am offering a brand new conception. Elements of it are in place, but the conception needs to be more forcefully articulated, along with specific guidelines for action.

The final chapter focuses on what to do to improve the situation. These 'Guidelines for action' are directed at three different parts of the problem. First, for incumbent heads is advice concerning 'What's worth fighting for?' Second, guidelines for action are formulated for governors and school system administrators. Third, I conclude with comments on the central role of perpetual learning.

1 THE NONRATIONAL

WORLD OF THE HEAD

How bad are things for the head?

> Despite all the attention on the head's leadership
> role in the 1980s, we appear to be losing ground, if
> we take as our measure of progress the presence of
> increasingly large numbers of highly effective,
> satisfied heads.

The current picture presents a serious problem if one
considers the cumulative and ever increasing expectations
being placed on heads. One vivid example has been
presented in a study of 137 heads and deputy heads in the
Toronto Board of Education (Edu-Con, 1984). In this work
several measures indicated the problem of overload. Respondents were asked to rate 11 major expectations (for

example, new programme demands, number of local priorities and directives, number of directives from the government, etc.) in terms of whether the expectation had increased, decreased, or remained the same in the last five years. On average, across all 11 dimensions, 90 per cent of the heads/deputy heads reported an increase in demands, with only 9 per cent citing a decrease.

The heads and deputy heads reported a number of specific major additions to their responsibilities. The five most frequently mentioned (by more than 50 per cent of the respondents) were the following new procedures or programmes:

- Teacher Performance Review
- Curriculum Implementation Plan
- Heritage Language Programme
- Identification, Placement Review Committee
- Appraisal for a Better Curriculum

Nineteen other additions were also mentioned. In response to a direct question, no one could think of a responsibility that had been 'removed'. Some 'reduction' was mentioned in teacher hiring due to declining enrolment. Time demands, as might be expected, were listed as having increased in dealing with parent and community groups (92 per cent said there was an increase), administration activities (88 per cent), staff involvement and student services (81 per cent) and social services (81 per cent). Parents, consultants, and teachers who were asked all confirmed that there were greater time and programme demands on heads over the past five years.

There was one other finding about expectations and demands: heads did not object to many of the new responsibilities *per se*. In fact, the majority saw value in such new programmes as the Curriculum Implementation Plan and the Teacher Performance Review Programme. They were concerned more with the complexity and time demands involved in implementing the new procedures than the procedures themselves.

time — biggest concern

Heads and deputy heads were also asked about their perceptions of effectiveness. Remarkably, in light of the fact that it is a self report, 61 per cent of the respondents reported a *decrease in effectiveness*, with only 13 per cent saying it was about the same, and 26 per cent reporting an increase. An identical percentage (61 per cent) reported decreases in 'the effectiveness of assistance ... from immediate superiors and from administration'. The list goes on: 84 per cent report a decrease in the authority of the head, 72 per cent a decrease in trust in the leadership of the head, and 76 per cent a decrease in head involvement in decision-making at the system level. On the question, 'Do you think the head can effectively fulfil all the responsibilities assigned to him/her?', 91 per cent responded, 'No'.

In the Ottawa Board of Education, 'The Committee On Overloading the Elementary Curriculum' (1984) drew the same conclusion about the curriculum itself. The committee concluded that the curriculum is constantly being expanded with little taken out, with the result that the quality of education is deteriorating because there is too much to cover.

Other studies indicate similar problems. Our own case studies of four medium-sized school boards in Ontario indicated that progress is very slow even with the help of Curriculum Review Development and Implementation models, and despite five to ten years' work improving the models in practice (Fullan *et al.*, 1986). Even in the board that had been at it the longest and had made considerable progress, it was estimated that less than 10 per cent of the heads were functioning as highly effective curriculum leaders.

> **Virtually every school board in Ontario has redrafted the role definition of heads over the past decade to make explicit that the head is expected to be the leader of school level implementation of policies and programmes.**

Leithwood and Montgomery's *The Principal Profile* (1986) is based on four levels of effectiveness, termed: the administrator, the humanitarian, the programme manager, and the systematic problem solver. The administrator focuses on regulations leaving professional matters to teachers; the humanitarian is concerned with climate and interpersonal relationships; the programme manager concentrates on curriculum planning and implementation of school board policies; and the problem solver focuses on student learning and any problems which stand in the way of increasing learning. Leithwood and Montgomery also estimate that less than 10 per cent of the heads in Ontario are in the category of problem solver. We have no reason to believe heads elsewhere fare better.

Accompanying the increased expectations for overall improvement, of course, has been a policy conclusion backed up by considerable research that the head is the chief agent of change and improvement at the school level. Virtually every school board in Ontario has redrafted the role definition of heads over the past decade to make explicit that the head is expected to be the leader of school level implementation of policies and programmes. I shall return to the question of the head and change, but first we should consider the matter of stability.

Conservative tendencies in the headship

I speak here not of official policies or official expectations. The question is whether in *practice* there are more tendencies toward conservatism than toward change in the orientation and actual carrying out of the role. Sarason (1982) and Lortie (1987), while writing about the American school head, provide some fundamental and provocative analyses in response to the question of conservatism.

Sarason (1982) starts with the observation that being a classroom teacher by itself is not a very good preparation for being an effective head. In their interaction with heads,

7

says Sarason, teachers (as future heads) obtain only a very narrow slice of what it means to be a head. This narrowness of experience is all the more constrained where the teacher's experience is limited to one or two schools. Next, the newly appointed deputy head or head often experiences emphasis on maintenance and stability from his or her teachers. Despite the fact that the head views his or her role as implying leadership, when resistance to recommendations or ideas for change are encountered, heads often respond in one of two ways. According to Sarason, they 'assert authority or withdraw from the fray' (1982: 160). This is, no doubt, an oversimplification, but Sarason's overall conclusion is that the narrowness of preparation and the demands for maintaining or restoring stability encourage heads to play it safe.

Lortie (1987) draws specifically on his study of suburban primary school heads in Chicago (which provides a narrow sample base) and, more generally on his observations of American education. Lortie claims that there are four powerful 'Built-in Tendencies Toward Stabilizing the Principal's Role', related to (1) recruitment and induction, (2) role constraints and psychic rewards, (3) the constraint of system standardization, and (4) career contingencies.

Concerning recruitment and induction, Lortie comments on the narrowness of experience and limited exposure to new ideas:

> Persons who have been exposed to a wide range of educational ideas and practices, and have seen those in actual use, are more likely to favor and, when influential, push for change; attachment to traditional ways is normally associated with isolation from alternative ways of doing things. If principals were cosmopolitans who had witnessed considerable variety in the course of their work lives, we might expect them to be advocates of change, to bring novel procedures and practices to their schools.
>
> (Lortie, 1987: 4)

[handwritten margin note: multiple experience vs a factor]

But, says Lortie, 'there is little to encourage us to so classify them, at least on the basis of the typical work experience and study found in our sample; the large majority have worked in a small number of distinct settings' (p. 4).

The second major conservative tendency Lortie identifies is 'role constraints and psychic rewards'. Elaborating on Sarason's point, Lortie states that heads consider the relationship with teachers to be the most salient within their role, and that when it comes to change, the relationship is problematic:

> If change can be costly for those who are asked to undertake it, it follows that subordinates will be most ready to change when the superordinate can argue, with some degree of plausibility, that there will be gains to offset any losses. This is particularly difficult to demonstrate in education as technical knowledge in the field is insufficiently well developed to provide a strong rationale for innovation, to convince teachers that the change will produce the increased learning which could serve as a source of additional work satisfaction.
>
> (Lortie, 1987: 7)

Heads considering a particular change face two questions. First, will students benefit if the changes are made? This is a difficult question to answer since change proposals are rarely accompanied by such evidence. Second, if teachers resist, is the potential loss of goodwill and influence on teachers worth the risk? Lortie predicts that given the probable answers to these questions heads will not push hard for change in their schools.

Third, Lortie talks about system standardization. He notes that three factors normally constrain the emergence of school individuality. The rationale of curricular integration, formal authority arrangements and pressures toward system-wide equity, all 'inhibit the impulse to innovate in individual elementary schools' (p. 11).

Career contingencies and system context is the last

theme taken up by Lortie. When asked what criteria superordinates were more likely to use in evaluating their performance, many heads placed emphasis on the opinions of parents and teachers. Lortie asks,

> What is the relationship between the introduction of change and the evocation of discontent? Is it not more likely that principals who challenge the status quo are more likely to agitate conservative parents and/or resistant teachers? Are persons who are pleased by a particular change, or indifferent to it, as likely to register their views with central office? When can a principal have confidence that his superordinates will make a clear distinction between justified complaints and the noise made by those who are simply irritated by the new?
>
> (Lortie, 1987: 12–13)

Lortie concludes that successful innovation, under the circumstances he describes, requires 'highly sophisticated managerial behavior' at both the system and school (head) levels; and that 'such talents are scarce in any organizational setting'.

Before one concludes that the 'big bad system' causes all evil, let us return to Sarason. He takes up the additional theme that people's conception of 'the system' governs what they do, even though it may be a correct or faulty conception. He states the problem bluntly:

> While I do not in any way question that characteristics of the system can and do have interfering effects on an individual's performance . . . 'the system' is frequently conceived by the individual in a way that obscures, many times unwittingly, the range of possibilities available to him or her. Too frequently the individual's conception of the system serves as a basis for inaction and rigidity, or as a convenient target onto which one can direct blame for most anything. The principal

illustrates this point as well or better than anyone else
in the school system.

(Sarason, 1982: 164)

Sarason then gives several examples of heads who were
using atypical procedures (for example, using older students to work with younger ones) in a school system, in
which other heads in the same system claimed would not
work successfully because the system would not allow it,
it was counter to policy, one would be asking for trouble,
etc. etc. Sarason suggests that the tendency for heads to
anticipate trouble from the system is one of the most
frequent and strong obstacles to trying new procedures.
Sarason makes three important observations in his
analysis:

> First, the knowledge on the part of the principal that
> what he or she wants to do may and will encounter
> frustrating obstacles frequently serves as justification
> for staying near the lower limits of the scope of the
> role. Second, the principal's actual knowledge of the
> characteristics of the system is frequently incomplete
> and faulty to the degree that his or her conception or
> picture of what the system will permit or tolerate leads
> the principal to a passive rather than an active role.
> Third, and perhaps most important, the range in
> practices among principals within the same system is
> sufficiently great as to suggest that the system permits
> and tolerates passivity and activity, conformity and
> boldness, dullness and excitement, incompetency and
> competency.

(Sarason, 1982: 171)

I am not suggesting that Lortie and Sarason have it
exactly right for the United States, let alone for elsewhere.
Recall, however, that they are speaking about tendencies;
that more times than not the head, whether for system or
individual reasons, will end up tolerating rather than doing
something about the status quo even when he or she

knows that improvements should be made. Whether or not they are precisely correct, they are right that there is something radically wrong. Despite all the attention on the head's leadership role in the 1980s, we appear to be losing ground, if we take as our measure of progress the presence of increasingly large numbers of highly effective, satisfied heads.

The head and change

> **I maintain that there are serious limitations to the current conception of the head as lead implementer of official policies and programmes, that existing research is being misinterpreted in fundamental ways and that at least a good part of the way we are going about it is unintentionally reinforcing dependency.**

The image of the head in research and policy literature has shifted in the past ten years from the head as 'gatekeeper' to head as 'instructional leader'. Planned change, school improvement, effective schools and staff development all bear the mark of the head as a key figure for leading and supporting change.[1] Hall and his colleagues state it flatly: 'the degree of implementation of the innovation is different in different schools because of the actions and concerns of the head' (Hall *et al*., 1980: 26). There are, of course, examples where change has occurred successfully without the head, and there are newer formulations which stress the importance of different teaming arrangements (Hall, 1987), but nearly everyone agrees that the head is or should be a driving force for improvement.

I maintain that there are serious limitations to the current conception of the head as lead implementer of official policies and programmes, that existing research is being misinterpreted in fundamental ways and that at least a good part of the way we are going about it is unintentionally reinforcing dependency.

To start rather simply, despite ten years of effort, heads as dynamic change agents are still empirically rare – probably fewer than one in ten. Is this simply a function of training, selection, and support on the job, not yet catching up to practice? Or do we have the wrong conception and/or are we going about it the wrong way?

Next, a great deal of the research, such as the findings on which we are basing new policies and expectations, is seriously limited in that it reports on what happens to single innovations. What a head does with one innovation does not necessarily predict what he or she will do with another one. In a study of what influences heads' behaviour, Trider and Leithwood (1988) found that the content background of heads (naturally enough) influenced how much attention and effort they put into particular policies. For example, a background in special education would predict the amount of attention given to new special education policies, but not necessarily to that given to a new science priority. We just cannot generalize from studies of single innovations.

Last and more fundamentally, the reality is that heads are not contending with individual innovations or even a series of innovations. They are in the business of attempting to manage multiple innovations. Until we have many more studies which examine holistically the inside-out picture of how the head does and could manage the 'field' of innovative possibilities facing him or her, we will be restricted in the conclusions we can draw. Nor do I believe, as will be discussed later, that the answer lies in implementing as many innovations as possible, among those that are 'supposed' to be implemented.

Some of the more recent studies attempt to go beyond the problem of focusing on single innovations. Hall and his colleagues (1987; Hord and Hall, 1987) describe three types of heads: initiators, managers, and responders. Initiators, for example, 'have clear, decisive long-range policies and goals that transcend, but include implementation of the current innovation'. However, the empirical base in their study of heads is a single innovation. We do not know whether, let alone how, these heads deal with multiple innovations.

Leithwood and Montgomery (1986) have gone the farthest of anyone in working out an elaborate, focused theoretical framework based on considerable research. *The Principal Profile*, as indicated above, identifies four levels of effectiveness. The authors detail the orientations, skills, and behaviours for each group according to the categories of decision-making, goals, factors, and strategies. Heads operating at the highest level of effectiveness – the problem solver – are preoccupied with impact and students and are systematic information processors toward that end.

There is no question that the conception of systematic problem solver meets the criterion of contending with multiple innovations in the service of valued educational goals, but there are some niggling questions. There are very few systematic problem solvers in the real world of education. Trider and Leithwood (1988) found none in their study of heads, so they were not able to report on what influences these high performing heads. Further, and this is hypothetical, when a system fixes on the Leithwood profile as the solution, does it generate more dependencies than it does systematic problem solvers? I do not refer to the intentions of the authors, or to the conception of the ideal head, but to how the profile is experienced by practising and would-be heads. The question is: does a well worked out profile in the hands of superordinates, who themselves may not be systematic problem solvers, create a sense of dependency among heads as they attempt to measure up?

It is not the profile *per se* that is in question, but rather the way in which external frameworks are used. There is the need to build in exposure to external criteria, and the profile is particularly good in this respect. The interdependent versus dependent head uses such external conceptions as a method for describing his or her own practices in relation to ideal practices, and for critically reflecting on and extending effectiveness.

The problem of dependency can be extended to the proliferation of Curriculum Review Development and Implementation (CRDI) models in Canada. These models typically come in the form of policies and procedures outlining the phases and steps toward effective implementation of selected priorities. In the short run at least, CRDI-type models represent additional burdens on the head. In addition to having to implement particular new policies, heads also have to follow the implementation procedures. Insult having been added to injury, heads now face a double innovation, for implementing the implementation plan *is* an innovation. Since most of these implementation procedures are not well-tested, 'debugged', or well-practised, things inevitably go wrong. They are procedures which are supposed to be followed and which can easily create a situation of dependency as heads strive to follow the plan. Recall that the 'Curriculum Implementation Plan' was one of the most frequently mentioned problems for the heads in the Toronto Board survey, even though they saw it as potentially valuable. Comparisons with the National Curriculum in England and Wales are obvious as heads react to the requirement for Local Management of Schools (LMS) plans, as well as to a host of other impositions.

To summarize and extend the main points of the last several pages:

1 Emphasizing innovation can be just as authoritarian and dependency-generating as emphasizing tradition.
2 Expecting heads to lead the implementation of all official policies, when the task is clearly impossible, creates overload, confusion, powerlessness, and dependency or cynicism.
3 Externally generated, top down procedures designed to

help may backfire as they add to overload, and may establish another external standard which has the head looking for the solution outside his or her own self and situation.

Highly refined procedures require great care and sophistication. Since the latter is in short supply in most social systems, perhaps we should not place too great a burden on the refinement of models and procedures. One of the reasons we need to look elsewhere is that 'it is not too rational out there'.

The nonrational world

> There is no point in lamenting the fact that the system is unreasonable, and no percentage in waiting around for it to become more reasonable. It won't.

As a bridge to new conceptions for the role of the head, the concept put forth by Patterson *et al.* (1986) of the non-rational world is particularly useful. The nonrational world is not a nonsensical one. Patterson and his colleagues suggest that organizations in today's society do not follow an orderly logic, but a complex one that is often paradoxical and contradictory, but nevertheless understandable and amenable to influence. They contrast the assumptions of the rational conception with those of a nonrational conception on five dimensions. First, goals: school systems are necessarily guided by multiple and sometimes competing goals. Second, power: power in school systems is distributed throughout the organization. Third, decision-making: decision-making is inevitably a bargaining process to arrive at solutions that satisfy a number of constituencies. Fourth, external environment:

the public influences school systems in major ways that are unpredictable. Fifth, teaching process: there are a variety of situationally appropriate ways to teach that are effective.

Patterson and colleagues state their basic position contrasting the rational and nonrational models:

> The central difference between the two models lies in their interpretation of reality. Proponents of the rational model believe that a change in procedures will lead to improvement in educational practice. In short the rational model begins with an 'if-then' philosophy. If A happens, then B will logically follow. When reality fails to validate this 'if-then' perspective (i.e., when B doesn't happen) the argument shifts to an 'if-only' position. If only schools will tighten up rules and regulations, improved discipline will follow. If only teachers are given clear directives, then improved teaching will follow. Advocates for the nonrational model claim that the 'if-then and if-only' model is wishful thinking; organizations do not always behave in a logical, predictable manner. Acknowledging this reality, the nonrational model attempts to turn it to the advantage of those in the system. Rather than spending organizational energy trying to conform to wishful thinking, the nonrational model allows us to invest our energy into devising solutions that will work, given reality.
>
> (Patterson *et al.*, 1986: 27)

Their own solution, which I draw on partly in the next section, is to develop three integrated strategies: (1) managing the organizational culture, (2) strategic planning, and (3) empowerment.

It is more reasonable, argue Patterson and his colleagues, that actions should be based on a conception of the way the world is. The reality is that educational policies get generated through a mixture of educational and political considerations. It will always be more complicated than we want. The message for the head, as for others, is that there is no point in lamenting the fact that the system is unreasonable, and no percentage in waiting around for it to become more reasonable. It won't.

We need to move away from the notion of how the head can become master implementer of multiple policies and programmes. What is needed is to reframe the question. What does a reasonable leader do, faced with impossible tasks? In the next section, I start by moving outside the educational literature to get at the answer. It is not that existing educational literature is unhelpful. Indeed educational literature contains many elements of the answer. It seems, however, more fruitful to step back and to start with even more basic ideas, because a new conception of the head's role is needed.

> **We need to move away from the notion of how the head can become master implementer of multiple policies and programmes. What is needed is to reframe the question. What does a reasonable leader do, faced with impossible tasks?**

Note

1 I have not elaborated on research references. Those who wish to review some of the material directly should see Barth (1986), Bossert *et al.* (1982), Fullan (1991), Hord and Hall (1987), Leithwood and Montgomery (1982, 1986), Manasse (1985). See also Cox *et al.* (1987) for an important perspective on the role of the head.

2 NEW CONCEPTIONS

OF THE HEADSHIP

> **Entrepreneurs exploit innovation.** (Drucker, 1985)

Heads are middle managers. As such, they face a classical organizational dilemma. Rapport with subordinates is critical as is keeping superordinates happy. The endless supply of new policies, programmes and procedures ensures that the dilemma remains active. The expectation that heads should be the leaders in the implementation of changes which they have had no hand in developing and may not understand is especially troublesome (Fullan, 1991). This becomes all the more irritating when those immediately above them also have not been involved in change development and may not fully understand the programmes either. What is needed is to return to the basics. What are the key concepts for the head of the

1990s? What are the essential skills and qualities required?

New concepts

There is a new conception of the middle manager emerging in the literature on modern successful innovative organizations. Bennis and Nanus (1985), Drucker (1985), Leavitt (1986), and Peters and Waterman (1982) are representative of the best authors of this literature.[1] These books tend to focus on top management and how these leaders should behave and how they should promote leadership in those middle managers below them.

It is Block (1987) who has brought these implications to a head for middle management in *The Empowered Manager*. He offers a conception which I believe is directly applicable to the headship. It is not a risk free way forward, but a potentially powerful one. In the next few pages, I will describe Block's analysis in some detail because it so clearly captures the types of problems typical of those experienced by heads and so convincingly points to the concepts suitable for solution.

Block talks about the quiet revolution in innovative organizations away from tighter controls, precisely defined jobs, and close supervision, towards the entrepreneurial spirit. This spirit is typified by responsibility, public accountability, interactive professionalism, and the recognition that playing positive politics is essential, possible, and the key to effectiveness. Using the concepts of entrepreneurial spirit and positive political skills, Block builds the case that it is possible for middle managers to shape if not create organizations that they believe in, even in the midst of the nonrational world.

Almost as if he were inside the school system, Block begins by stating: 'At the deepest level, the enemy of high performing systems is the feeling of helplessness that so many of us in organizations seem to experience' (p. 1).

Political skill means making improvements in organizations in a way that maintains and enhances the support of those above and below us. Block cuts right to the fundamental issue early:

> The core of the bureaucratic mind-set is not to take responsibility for what is happening. Other people are the problem . . . Reawakening the original spirit means we have to confront the issue of our own autonomy. To pursue autonomy in the midst of a dependency-creating culture is an entrepreneurial act.
>
> (Block, 1987: 6)

Block describes individuals using politics in a traditional, hierarchical organization as becoming good at:

- manipulating situations and at times people,
- managing information and plans carefully to our own advantage,
- invoking the names of high level people when seeking support for our projects.
- becoming calculating in the way we manage relationships,
- paying great attention to what the people above him or her want from us,
- living with the belief that in order to get ahead, we must be cautious in telling the truth.

> (Block, 1987: 9)

He then challenges, 'Why get better at a bad game?' We need to get better, says Block, in being positively political 'as an act of service, contribution, and creation' (p. 9).

The fundamental choices according to Block are between maintenance and greatness, between caution and courage and between dependency and autonomy.

Maintenance includes being preoccupied with playing it safe. It means holding on to what we have and not risking making mistakes. Mistakes are frowned on more than achievements are rewarded. Choosing greatness ups the stakes. Mere improvement is not good enough, says Block.

Related to maintenance is caution: the message of bureaucracies is to be careful. Performance reviews and implementation plans may symbolize the pressure to be careful, even though they are frequently intended to produce the opposite. To confront an issue when others are acting as if there is no issue is an act of courage.

Organizations that say they value autonomy and then look for conformity foster a dependency mentality. Block (1987: 15) asserts: 'Autonomy is the attitude that my actions are my own choices and the organization I am a part of is in many ways my own creation.' He continues:

We hear people constantly calling for strong leadership. Everyone is waiting for top management to get its act together. When is top management going to give vision and direction to this organization? We focus a great deal on supervisory style and say with certainty that the supervisor sets the tone for how other people behave . . . All of these wishes for changes above us are examples of our dependency. They all imply that until something above me changes, do not expect me to operate much differently . . .

The price we pay for dependency is our own sense of helplessness. Helplessness and waiting for clear instructions before acting are the opposite of the entrepreneurial spirit . . . I must confront my own wish for dependency and move in the direction of autonomy . . . When we choose autonomy we realise that there is nothing to wait for . . .

I can now get on with the business of serving my users and customers and managing a unit in a way that expresses my own personal values about how organizations should work. If the people in power above do not like what I am doing, let them stop me. Better to proceed than to wait for direction. Better to ask forgiveness than permission. Better to be seen as stubborn than incompetent.

(Block, 1987: 16–17)

Block concludes his introduction to the topic by acknowledging that there are times when it is necessary to play it safe, such as when we are new on the job and our knowledge is limited; when the organization is under attack and survival is at stake; when we have just gone through considerable risk; and when there is zero trust in the environment. These conditions notwithstanding, the message from Block is that we play it safe far too often, echoing Sarason's (1982) observations reported earlier that heads' conceptions of the 'system' needlessly limit what they can do. Acting autonomously and with initiative has elements of risk, but it is one of the few ways of breaking the cycle. In many circumstances, people find that autonomous action, when tried, is tolerated and even rewarded.

Block then talks about developing antidotes for bureaucracy. He acknowledges that if top executives support your efforts, it is much easier, but states flatly: '. . . the power of position is overrated. We frequently find people near or at the top feeling as powerless as people at the middle or the bottom' (p. 59).

Developing the idea of antidotes further, Block explains five rules of 'Enlightened Self-Interest':

1 Meaning
2 Contribution and service
3 Integrity
4 Positive impact on others' lives
5 Mastery

Meaning is reflected in the decision that I will engage in activities that have meaning to me or us, and are genuinely needed. Contribution and service involves the decision to do the things that seriously contribute to the organization and its purpose. Integrity as Block defines it:

> essentially means to put into words what we see happening, to tell people what is really going on within our unit and what we see going on outside our unit.

> Integrity isn't a moral issue . . . It is more the issue of whether it is possible for us to tell the truth about what we see happening, to make only those promises we can deliver on, to admit to our mistakes, and to have the feeling that the authentic act is always the best for the business.
>
> (Block, 1987: 83)

Positive impact on others' lives suggests that in the long run it is in our self-interest to treat other people well. And, mastery, 'the final component of enlightened self-interest is the goal of simply learning as much as you can about the activity that you're engaged in . . . Learning and performance are intimately related.' Block summarizes his analysis in these powerful words:

> The key to positive politics, then, is to look at each encounter as an opportunity to support autonomy and to create an organization of our own choosing. It requires viewing ourselves as the primary instrument for changing the culture. Cultures get changed in a thousand small ways, not by dramatic announcements emanating from the boardroom. If we wait until top management gives leadership to the change we want to see, we miss the point. For us to have any hope that our own preferred future will come to pass, we provide the leadership. We hope that the world around us supports our vision, but even if it doesn't, we will act on that vision. Leadership is the process of translating intentions into reality.
>
> (Block, 1987: 97–8)

Politics at its best is 'where our actions, not our speeches, become our political statement' (p. 98). We will return to Block in Chapter 3 for some advice on 'what's worth fighting for?' In the meantime, he has given us an orientation, some basic concepts or a better way of thinking about the problem. The issue is not the bureaucratic one of how to implement everything that is supposed to be implemented; it is finding one's meaningful place among the multiplicity of choices. Entrepreneurs exploit innovation (Drucker, 1985).

Patterson, Purkey and Parker's (1986) discussion of educational leadership for a nonrational world echoes Block's conclusions. We cannot wait for the system to become more rational because it just will not happen. We cannot wait for those above us to become enlightened because it happens too infrequently and more importantly it looks for the solution in the wrong place. Patterson *et al.* identify three key concepts or strategies for addressing the situation: managing the organizational culture, strategic planning, and empowerment. For the first – organizational culture – they stress the importance of identifying and articulating the guiding beliefs of the school. These beliefs are the values and mission, with respect to both what is and what should be. The authors provide an illustrative set of guiding beliefs under ten principles: principles of purpose, of empowerment, of decision-making, of belonging, of trust and confidence, of excellence, of recognition and reward, or caring, of integrity, and of diversity (Patterson *et al.*, 1986: 50–1). Once identified, the central questions are: 'Are the guiding beliefs still desirable? Are the guiding beliefs desirable but not clearly understood, or perhaps misinterpreted? Are the guiding beliefs all right, but the daily behavior doesn't coincide with the values?' (Patterson *et al.*, 1986: 55)

The second core concept offered by Patterson and his colleagues is strategic planning. Table 1, reproduced from Patterson *et al.* (1986: 56), summarizes the features of strategic planning for a nonrational world, as they see it.

Thus, strategic planning focuses on the external environment as well as the internal organization; it fosters cross-cutting relationships to obtain greater access to resources and ideas; it works with medium- and short-range goals in recognition of the fact that the external environment is ever changeable and active. Because of the uncertain nature of the nonrational world, strategic

Table 1

Category	Conventional planning	Strategic planning
World view	Internal	External
System perspective	Segmental	Integrated
Planning horizon	Long range	Medium/short range
Data base	Quantitative	Qualitative
Outcome	Master plan	Masterful planning

planning relies on subjective judgement, intuition, and other qualitative indicators as much as on quantitative data; in contrast to the long-range masterplan, strategic planning's goal is 'to produce a stream of wise decisions designed to achieve the mission of the organization' accepting that 'the final product may not resemble what was initially intended' (p. 61). They offer three techniques for conducting strategic planning – environmental analysis, internal analysis, and integration of the two for purposes of action.

Empowerment is the third major concept. In addition to reinforcing the need for taking steps toward self-empowerment, Patterson *et al.* (1986) discuss the leaders' role in empowering others (such as head to teacher), and empowerment through alliances with sponsors, peers, and subordinates which can be especially productive.

One final set of compatible concepts comes from Bennis and Nanus' (1985) study of 90 top leaders. These writers conclude that effective leaders employ four basic strategies:

- Attention through vision
- Meaning through communication
- Trust through positioning
- The deployment of self

Bennis and Nanus state that 'the new leader . . . is one who commits people to action, who converts followers into leaders, and who may convert leaders into agents of change' (1985: 3). Focusing on the four strategies, Bennis and Nanus first describe vision:

Management of attention through *vision* is the creating of focus. What we discovered is that leaders also *pay attention* as well as catch it . . . the new leadership under discussion is not arbitrary or unilateral but rather an impressive and subtle sweeping back and forth of energy . . .

In all these cases, the leader may have been the one who chose the image from those available at the moment, articulated it, gave it form and legitimacy, and focussed attention on it, but the leader only rarely was the one who conceived it in the first place . . . therefore, the leader must be a superb listener; successful leaders are *great askers*, and they do pay attention.

(pp. 28, 32 and 96, original emphasis)

Meaning through communication is a second essential element and encompasses the capacity to influence and organize meaning for the members of the organization: 'Getting the message across unequivocally at every level is an absolute key . . . Leadership through communication is the creation of understanding, participation and ownership of the vision' (pp. 39, 112 and 143).

Bennis and Nanus make it clear that developing commitment to new visions requires constant communications and a variety of other methods including training, recruitment criteria, new policies and so forth.

As for *trust* Bennis and Nanus offer this:

people trust people who are predictable, whose positions are known and who keep at it; leaders who are trusted make themselves known, make their positions clear.

(p. 44)

Bennis and Nanus state two critical reasons for stressing trust through positioning:

> The first relates to organizational integrity – having a clear sense of what it stands for. The second is related to constancy on staying the course. Positioning involves creating a niche in a complex changing environment through persistence, integrity, and trust.
>
> (p. 3)

The deployment of self through positive self regard consists of three components according to Bennis and Nanus:

> ... knowledge of one's strengths, the capacity to nurture and develop those strengths, and the ability to discern the fit between one's strengths and weaknesses and the organization's needs.
>
> (pp. 61–2)

They also observe that such leaders induce positive 'other-regard'. Effective leaders set high standards but they also use five key skills according to Bennis and Nanus: the ability to accept people as they are; the capacity to approach relationships and problems in terms of the present rather than the past; the ability to treat those who are close to them with the same courteous attention that they would extend to strangers and casual acquaintances (Bennis and Nanus cite two particular problems of over-familiarity – not hearing what is said and failing to provide feedback indicating attentiveness); the ability to trust others even if the risk is great; and the ability to do without constant approval and recognition from others (pp. 66–7).

All the leaders in the Bennis and Nanus study were perpetual learners. They had learned how to learn in an organizational context (p. 189). They constantly learned on the job and enabled and stimulated others to learn.

As I said before, I have deliberately drawn on literature outside the vast and growing body of work on the head. There are, of course, many elements in the writings on headship which compare unfavourably and favourably to the concepts discussed here. Relative to unfavourable comparisons, approaches which have the narrow target of student achievement alone, and competency based schemes engineered in great detail by superordinates, are antithetical to the new conception of middle managers. (See Duke's useful analysis on broadening the indicators for assessing school heads (1985).) These approaches are doomed to failure except in the limited sense of sometimes boosting achievement scores in the short run on a few tests. They create excessive narrowness and dependency. People employing such approaches win the odd battle, but the war is lost in contending with the multiple demands of the nonrational world.

Many elements compatible with the new conceptions are also to be found in the literature. Leithwood's idea of the systematic problem solver is the empowered middle manager. Barth's well-known work at the Harvard Principals' Center provides another solid example. Barth says, 'I am convinced that the greatest opportunities for the professional development of teachers reside under the schoolhouse roof and that the principal can be a powerful force in assisting teacher growth' (1986: 482). The role of the head in the professionalization of teaching at the school level is another face of the empowered middle manager. The main limitation to Leithwood's, Barth's, and other similar work is that they would benefit from a grounding in the core organizational concepts discussed in this section. Without such fundamental grounding, the current work on headship runs the risk of either unwittingly contributing to dependency or at the least not providing the most powerful conceptual leverage for getting at the heart of the problem.

We can now round out the analysis by considering the 'skills and qualities' side of the coin.

> **Heads should be able to explain themselves.**

Skills and qualities

In another study, we examined the role of supervisory officers in Ontario (Fullan *et al.*, 1987b). Among other things, we identified the skills and qualities perceived to be vital by supervisory officers to be effective in their work. We grouped the responses in the following clusters:

- Communication (oral, written, listening)
- Human Relations (empathy, interpersonal relations, motivation, human development, conflict management)
- Integrity
- Knowledge
- Organization
- Persistence and Stamina
- Planning (analysis, implementation, evaluation)
- Political Astuteness
- Self Confidence
- Vision

The head, I would contend, needs precisely these same skills. Without getting into a detailed treatment, it is useful to align some of the main concepts we have been discussing with their corresponding skills and qualities. Table 2 provides such a summary.

The concepts and skills form a set. For example, it is not any autonomy that will do, but autonomy in combination with the other six characteristics such as internal-to-the-school and external-to-the-school interdependence. In essence, the new conception of the head is one where school-based decision-making is basic, but it is in the service of shared visions and goals for the school, and is dynamically plugged into the immediate environment of the school system. If possible, depending on the leadership at the system level it should have rapport with the system. School-based decision-making, under these circumstances, means to be relatively autonomous, but to be

Table 2 Essential concepts and skills/qualities of the new head

Concept	Illustrative skills/qualities
Vision/greatness	integrity, listening skills, knowledge, values, analytic powers
Autonomy	initiative, internal locus of control
Courage	risk taking, values, integrity
Meaning and empowerment in others: internal to the school	communication skills (listening, writing, speaking), extension of values of autonomy, human relations
Meaning and empowerment in others: external to the school	communication, analysis, political astuteness, human relations
Strategic planning	analysis, human relations
Deployment of self	integrity, self-confidence, persistence, perpetual learning

interdependent, as, for example, through frequent two-way communication with the system. Heads should be able to explain themselves. They need to be influential in presenting their plans and ideas to the system in order to obtain the external legitimacy and resources necessary for substantial success.

The concepts presented in this section are above all a way of thinking about the organization. Heads need techniques and skills in order to be effective. But no amount of sophistication and skills can resolve the impossible. Developing a better way of thinking about the role is a more fundamental resource for tackling the nonrational world.

A word of caution

If heads really became as good as these concepts call for them to be they would be rather scary. There is a bit too much of the great leader theory built into the notion of managerial empowerment. However, given all the inherent tendencies repressing the head's role, there is not much danger that many will go over the top of the scale to some superhuman pinnacle. Significant movement toward the implementation of the core concepts is desirable provided that we are not seeking the leader as saviour. Second, the logical extension of managerial empowerment is teacher (and student and parent) empowerment (see Fullan *et al.*, 1987a). This does not mean giving over the reins of power to anyone who will take them. Effective managerial power includes, by definition, the ability to empower, sometimes by freeing up, and often times by propelling, others within the organization. Ultimately, it will be the collective and subcollective professionalism of individual teachers and individual schools that will determine quality in education.

The question of what's worth fighting for must be addressed and acted upon immediately – today, tomorrow, next week.

Note

1 Tom Peters' book *Thriving on Chaos: Handbook for a Management Revolution* (1987) corroborates in forceful language, many of the basic premises presented here. Peters formulates five sets of prescriptions: creating total customer responsiveness, pursuing fast-paced innovation, achieving flexibility by empowering people, learning to love change, and building systems for a world turned upside down.

3 GUIDELINES FOR

ACTION

> **The starting point for what's worth fighting for is
> not system change, not change in others around us,
> but change in ourselves.**

To be practical, three areas of action are required simultaneously. First, in the short and continuing long run, a higher proportion of incumbent heads must take charge. The question of what's worth fighting for must be addressed and acted upon immediately – today, tomorrow, next week. Second, and in the mid-run, school systems must take action to create, insist on, support and be responsive to the conditions for school-based action – not in isolation, but as part of a visible, interactive network of public commitment to actual and acknowledged improvement. Third, in the short and long run, heads and those working with them must foster perpetual learning.

What's worth fighting for?

Block (1987) tells the story of consulting with a large supermarket chain in the United States in which one of the main goals was to shift decision-making to the level of store managers, much as some school systems have attempted to move toward greater school-based decision-making. The company had done a number of things (role clarification, training, communication meetings, and so forth) to try to shift power to the store manager and experienced little success. In assessing the situation, the common complaint was that the chain could not expect store managers to change their role without active day-to-day support of the district managers. Work with district managers was incorporated, but it too failed to make much of a difference. At that point, divisional managers were cited as creating or being a possible barrier. Division managers received attention with still only small improvements. A meeting was then scheduled with the President. While he had endorsed all the efforts to change, it was felt that perhaps he as well should be the target of change. His complaint was that he too was in the middle, because he found it difficult to please those above him, because he felt helpless to influence, on any scale, those below him. When all was said and done years of organizational development efforts across the different levels resulted in very slow movement toward the goal.

The point of the supermarket story is not that some organizations are better than others, or that everything is related to everything else. The story illustrates four very important issues related to our pursuit.

1 There is a tendency to externalize the problem, and to look for blockages at other levels of the system. Whether this is true or not in a given situation is irrelevant to the main point: waiting for others to act differently results in inaction and playing it safe.

2 There is an assumption that the entire 'system' must be

changed before improvements will occur – a chicken and egg stance which also immobilizes people.

3 Almost everyone perceives themselves to be in the 'middle' in some way, in the sense that there are people above them expecting more, and people below them who are immune to influence.

4 Everyone has some power, most often used *not* to do things.

All of this is to say that the starting point for what's worth fighting for is not system change, not change in others around us, but change in ourselves. This is both more achievable and paradoxically is the first step toward system change because it contributes actions not words.

Ten guidelines for individual action can be suggested. It is essential that these guidelines be viewed in concert, not as actions isolated from one another.

1 Avoid 'if only' statements, externalizing the blame and other forms of wishful thinking.

2 Start small, think big. Don't overplan or overmanage.

3 Focus on something concrete and important like curriculum and instruction.

4 Focus on something fundamental like the professional culture of the school.

5 Practise fearlessness and other forms of risk taking.

6 Empower others.

7 Build a vision relevant to both goals and change processes.

8 Decide what you are *not* going to do.

9 Build allies.

10 Know when to be cautious.

1 Avoid 'if only' statements

In most cases, 'if only' statements beg the question, externalize the blame, and immobilize people. If only the governors were better leaders, if only more resources were allocated to professional development, if only the DES would stop issuing so many policy changes and so forth. All of these wishes for changes around us, according to Block, are expressions of dependency and foster a sense of helplessness. As Block sums it up, 'waiting for clear instructions before acting is the opposite of the entre-preneurial spirit' (p. 16). Another way of putting it is, 'What can I do that is important to me and those around me?' Guideline 1, then, stresses the necessity for moving concretely in the direction of autonomy. In the first instance, what's worth fighting for is more of an internal battle than an external one.

Striving for complexity in the absence of action can generate more clutter than clarity.

---

2   Start small, think big. Don't overplan or overmanage

Complex changes (and managing multiple innovations in schools does represent complexity) means facing a para-dox. On the one hand, the greater the complexity, the greater the need to address implementation planning; on the other hand, the greater the thoroughness of implemen-tation planning the more complex the change process becomes. I talk later in guidelines 3 and 4 about what to focus on and in 7 about the need for a vision of the change process, but at this point it seems necessary to caution against overplanning and overmanaging. As Curriculum Review, Development and Implementation (CRDI) models become more prevalent, we should shift our concern to worrying about the problem of 'implementing the implementation plan'. After a certain amount of goal and priority setting, it is important not to get bogged down in elaborate needs assessment, discussion of goals and the like. Striving for complexity in the absence of action can generate more clutter than clarity. Effective managers have the capacity to short circuit potentially endless discussion and wheel-spinning by getting to the action.

Recent evidence in both business and education indicates that effective leaders have 'a bias for action'. They have an overall sense of direction, and start into action as soon as possible establishing small scale examples, adapting, refining, improving quality, expanding, and reshaping as the process unfolds (see, for example, Miles' work of 1987). This strategy might be summed up as start small: think big: or the way to get better at implementation planning is more by doing than by planning. Ownership is something that is developed through the process rather than in advance. Opportunities for reflection and problem solving are more important during the process than before it begins. In this sense, innovations are not things 'to be implemented', but are catalysts, points of departure or vehicles for examining the school and for making improvements.

For complex changes, tighter forms of planning and managing lose on two counts. They place the head in a dependent role, however unintended, and they hamper the extension of autonomy to teachers and to the school as a collectivity. Shared control over implementation at the school level is essential.

> **Consistency in schools must be obtained at the receiving end not the delivery end.**

3   Focus on something concrete and important like curriculum and instruction

Here we become involved in setting priorities and questions of consistency as in guideline 7. Priorities are generated through a mixture of political and educational merit. The result, as we have seen, is overload. The best way for a head to approach situations of impossible overload is to take the stance that 'we are going to implement a few things especially well, and implement other priorities as well as we would have anyway which is to keep them from getting out of hand'. Thus, there is not a call for any new neglect. This guideline assumes that within the array of policy priorities, there are 'some things' which can productively be examined and improved. It takes policies not as all things to be implemented, but as some things to be exploited. What's worth fighting for, is to select one area or a few instructional areas of major interest and/or need, and intensely pursue them through implementation. For example, a serious attack on an important curriculum area for the school represents a strike for something that is close to the core educational goals of schools even if all potential priorities are not being addressed. Such a positive initiative can be pointed to as an example of commitment and accomplishment in spite of the overload that surrounds schools.

Moreover, there is much greater choice in what can be done than is normally acknowledged. In terms of ends, there are many policy priorities from which one can choose to emphasize. Within selected priority directions, the means of implementation can vary widely. For most policies it is more accurate to treat policy implementation as an opportunity to define and develop the policy further, than it is to conceive of it as putting into practice someone else's ideas. Heads, in effect, have enormous leeway in practice.

Consistency provides sustenance for setting priorities. The combination of overload and frequent, seeming shifts in policy results in a *de facto* eclecticism. Consistency in schools must be obtained at the receiving end not the delivery end. Local and state politics are the bane of sustained follow-through. Learning accrues in a school whose staff have 'a constructed, continuous shared reality'.

Learning power comes from the consistent messages that students get about what it is to be an independent learner . . . a problem solver . . . a reader . . . a writer, and so forth. Conversely, schools that are eclectic in their approaches to learning (and the 'system' makes it easy to be eclectic) do poorly in terms of independent learning behaviours and achievement. It makes a lot of sense when you think about it, that if the expectations are changed every year then strong, successful learning is not going to accrue. If the head does not take charge, schools will be of this eclectic variety. Hence, mediocrity will prevail over excellence. The overwhelmed head yields to dependency. The focused head insists on consistency with purpose.

4 Focus on something fundamental like the professional culture of the school

In addition to concrete curriculum projects, the head must pay attention to the professional culture of the school. The general notion is the evolution of a school, where, by virtue of being on the staff, teachers would actually become better at their work.

We know that professional cultures, with their openness to new ideas, the giving and the receiving of help, collegiality focused on instructional improvement – are strongly related to success of implementation. It is possible to work on professional cultures directly, but it seems to me that doing it through curriculum projects, as in guideline 3, is more effective. Thus, curriculum projects would have a dual goal – one to implement the curriculum, and two to improve the interactive professionalism of teachers who participate in the project. To state it in another way, professional interactionism is both a strategy and an outcome. Fostering coaching and other forms of ongoing inservice should form a central part of any head's priorities. When all is said and done in relation to a given project, one of the outcomes should be a greater sense of critical collegiality and professionalism among teachers. Each project, in other words, should increase the skill and willingness of teachers to work together on school improvements. Empowerment, as explained in guideline 6, and vision building (guideline 7) are closely related to developing professional cultures of schools.

5   Practise fearlessness

Sarason (1982) described how some heads were carrying out certain practices at the same time that other heads in the same system were saying it was not allowed. How do they get away with it? It is somewhat superficial to say, but nonetheless true, that 'they just do it'.

Block (1987: 178ff) claims that many people take 'safe paths' in complex situations, such as believing simply in rationality, imitating others, or following the rules. He puts forward the idea that improvements are made through 'facing organizational realities' by 'continual acts of courage'. He suggests that if one is guided by vision building, as outlined in guideline 7, three 'acts' are necessary: (1) 'facing the harsh reality,' (2) examining 'our own contribution to the problem' and (3) making 'authentic statements in the face of disapproval'.

The tough version of acts of courage entails acting on something important, in such a way that we are 'almost indifferent to the consequences it might have for us' (p. 182). Like most risk taking, we have to be prepared to lose before we can win. Paradoxically, effective heads, as the research literature indicates, are men and women who take independent stances on matters of importance, and in most cases are all the more respected for it. At a less dramatic level, I would suggest that fearlessness can be practised on a modest scale. Three criteria for beginning might be to be selective, to do it on a small scale and to make a positive rather than a negative act of courage. So, for example, one might make it clear that the latest curriculum directive cannot be immediately addressed because the staff are in the midst of implementing another important priority. Then the head can demonstrate willingness to discuss the importance and progress of this other priority. Another example might be presenting a well worked out plan, asking for modest resources to implement something important to the school and the community.

There is such a thing as occupational suicide and no doubt there are many courageous acts that could be classified as foolish. But given the cautionary tendencies described in earlier sections, it seems legitimate to suggest that an increase in selective acts of fearlessness in reference to a major school goal would be a good thing.

6   Empower others

As a safeguard against being wrong and because it is essential for implementing serious improvements in any case, empowering others in the school has to form a major component of the effective head's agenda. It is becoming clearer in the research literature that complex changes in education may require active (top-down or external) initiation, but if they are to go anywhere, there must be a good deal of shared control and decision-making during implementation.

From their current research Miles (1987) and others analyse the successful evolution of effective secondary school programmes. In addition to several other factors, many of which are related to other items on our list, Miles stresses that while initiative often comes from the head, 'power sharing' is critical from that point onward. Successful schools were characterized by heads who supported and stimulated initiative-taking by others, who set up cross-hierarchical steering groups consisting of teachers, administrators, and sometimes parents and students and who delegated authority and resources to the steering group, while maintaining active involvement in or liaison with the groups.

As Patterson and his colleagues (1986) state, people become empowered when they can count on the support of the 'boss', can make or influence decisions affecting them and have access to information and resources enabling them to implement decisions. The authors (1986: 75–6) discuss the dilemma of leadership versus delegation. Too much freedom often results in a vague sense of direction and wasted time; clearly defined structure, on the other hand, often generates resistance or mechanical acceptance. In a statement that applies both to the relationship of school systems to schools, as well as head to teachers, Patterson and colleagues state:

> Senior officials must strike a balance between giving up total control of the group and holding too tightly to the reins. Delegation, in its optimal sense, means initially setting the parameters, then staying involved through coordinating resources, reviewing progress reports, and being able to meet teams at critical junctures.
>
> (1986: 76)

Three other points should be added to the concept of interactive power sharing within the school. First, this is not an individualistic exercise. It is a matter of creating groups responsible for and working on significant tasks. Such peer and hierarchical groups function to integrate both pressure and support to get things done. As it turns out, peer interaction represents a far more powerful form of pressure than traditional hierarchical forms.

Second, empowerment means additional resources, such as time, money, and personnel. The head must be able to deliver resources. Sometimes, but not always, he or she does this with extra money. Most times, by helping to invent imaginative ways for freeing up time. Effective heads do the latter all the time, and in ways which other heads either would not think of, or would say could not be done. Another finding of the research is that a little bit of time and resources, available regularly, can go a long way.

Third, it is important to reinforce the notion of the administrative team. Mortimore *et al.* (1988) traced the performance of 2000 students in 50 primary schools over a period of five years. The study represents one of the few, if not only, longitudinal studies of effective schools including the use of a series of premeasures, followed by a monitoring system over the five-year period. Among other results, it was found that in schools in which the deputy heads were actively involved in programme issues along with the heads, there was greater student achievement and teacher effectiveness than in schools in which the head acted as a more autonomous figure. Hall (1987) and his group, after starting with the assumption that the head was central as a change agent, concluded that it was the 'Change Facilitating Team' that was critical. In each successful case, they found a second, third, or fourth change agent (deputy head, departmental head or other manager) and that it was the 'team' that made the difference.

Finally, a more radical notion is that the ultimate extension of empowerment places teachers as central to professional decision-making in the school (Fullan and Connelly, 1987).

7   Build a vision relevant to both goals and change processes

Vision building feeds into and is fed by all other guidelines in this section. It cuts through the tendency to blame others; it provides a sense of direction for starting small but thinking big; it provides focus; it checks random fearlessness; it gives content to empowerment and alliance discussions; it gives direction for deciding what not to do. Above all, it permeates the enterprise with values, purpose, and integrity for both the what and the how of improvement.

Block and Patterson and colleagues provide examples of guiding beliefs or visions: we act as partners with our customers; we choose quality over speed; we want to understand the impact of our actions on our customers; we want consistency between our plans and action; we value high standards and expectations in our district; we support the decentralization of decisions as close to the point of implementation as possible, and so on. These basic values guide specific priorities (such as, every child in this school will concentrate on good writing) and are translated into consistent day-to-day actions over time.

The vital role of vision appears in every book on educational and organizational excellence. It is not an easy concept with which to work, largely because its formation, implementation and shaping in specific organizations is a constant process. An organization, to be effective, needs both a vision of the nature or content that it represents, and a clear vision of the processes it characteristically values and follows.

Vision is not something that someone happens to have; it is a much more fluid process and does not have to be – indeed it must not be – confined to a privileged few. In a real sense, implementation of any policy will be superficial unless all implementers come to have a deeply held version of the meaning and the importance of the change for them.

To start with the leader, Bennis and Nanus make it quite clear that top leaders in their study had, but did not invent, visions for their organizations. Indeed, these leaders were more likely to be good at extracting and synthesizing images from a variety of sources:

> All of the leaders to whom we spoke seemed to have been masters at selecting, synthesizing, and articulating an appropriate vision of the future . . . If there is a spark of genius in the leadership function at all, it must

lie in this transcending ability, a kind of magic, to assemble – out of all the variety of images, signals, forecasts and alternatives – a clearly articulated vision of the future that is at once single, easily understood, clearly desirable, and energizing.

(Bennis and Nanus, 1985: 101)

Vision building, then, is very much of an interactive process and is heavily dependent on two-way communication skills, empathy and exposure to a variety of ideas and stimuli. Patterson and colleagues state: 'Vision is the product of exercising many skills in a holistic way to create a mental picture of what the future could and should look like' (1986: 88). They claim further that there are four dimensions involved: foresight, hindsight, depth perception (seeing the big picture, its parts, and understanding how it really works) and peripheral vision (constantly scanning and processing the environment). Ideas as well as values are essential to vision.

Vision must be something arguably of value. It should be somewhat lofty or uplifting. It should have some concreteness. Leithwood and Montgomery's (1986) 'image of the educated learner'. and what it means to achieve that image provides one good example. Block emphasizes that 'creating a vision forces us to take a stand for a preferred future' (1987: 102). Vision also must withstand the marketplace and therefore has to make a contribution to what is important for significant others. Focusing on the clients, parents and children, and connecting with others in the organization to formulate an image of what we want for the future, begins the process of transcending the present. Block identifies several positive effects arising from putting our vision into work:

1 In an implicit way, it signifies our disappointment with what exists now. To articulate our vision of the future is to come out of the closet with our doubts about the organization and the way it operates, our doubts about the way our unit serves its customers, and our doubts

about the way we deal with each other inside the organization.

2 The vision exposes the future that we wish for our unit and opens us up to potential conflict with the visions of other people. We know in our hearts that visions are not negotiable, and therefore we run the risk of conflicting visions when we put them into words with each other.

3 Articulating a vision of greatness also forces us to hold ourselves accountable for acting in a way that is congruent with that vision. The vision states how we want to work with customers and users, and the vision states how we want to work with each other. Once we have created a vision and communicated it to the people around us, it becomes a benchmark for evaluating all of our actions.

(Block, 1987: 105)

We normally think of vision as something in the future, but we do not necessarily think in terms of how to get to that vision. When we do address the how, it is often formulated in a top-down manner – form a task force, clarify the vision, communicate and train it, assess it, etc. etc. As we now turn more directly to the aspects of process, a number of other dimensions must be introduced. Working on one's own vision is the starting point. The extension of this position is that it is the task of each person of the organization, to a certain extent, to create their own version of the vision of the future. Obviously, interactive professionalism will result in commonalities. Visions will tend to converge, if the guidelines in this section are followed. This will sometimes result in sharper differences but the more serious problem seems to be the absence of clearly articulated visions, not a multiplicity of them.

Dealing with the problem of 'what if we don't have a vision', Block makes a number of suggestions. He starts by saying that a vision statement is an expression of optimism or at least hope. Potential visions exist within most of us, even if they have not been put into words. If the question,

'Suppose you had a vision of greatness for this school, what would it be?' generates no response, Block maintains that this is an expression of despair and reluctance to take responsibility. Block continues by outlining some steps for coaching others in creating their own vision:

1 Pick an important project on which you are working and about which you care and with which you are frustrated. Describe the goals of the project and why you are frustrated.

2 Next ask why you care so much about the project. Your frustration is an expression of your commitment. If you were not so committed to a project, you would not be so frustrated. We ask people why they care so much about the project as a way of getting at their deeper values about their work. We all have strong values about doing work that has meaning, being of real service to our customers, treating other people well, and maintaining some integrity in the way we work. Keep asking 'Why?' 'Why?' 'Why?' until you hear some statements that seem to come from the heart.

3 Ask what your ideal way of working with your customers looks like. If you revisited your unit three years from now and greatness had been achieved, what would you see happening with customers?

4 Now ask the same questions about the future focussing on how you think people should treat each other in the unit.

(Block, 1987: 123–4)

The dialogue about vision, according to Block, should strive to achieve three qualities: depth, clarity, and responsibility relative to the vision. Depth is the degree to which the vision statement is personally held. Clarity comes from insisting on specific images. Vagueness, says Block, 'is a way of not making a commitment to a vision' (p. 124). Responsibility involves moving from helplessness to active ownership: 'the primary reason we demand that people create a vision statement is to reinforce the belief that all of us are engaged in the process of creating this organization' (p. 124).

It cannot be overemphasized that this guideline incorporates commitment to both the *content* of vision and to the *process* of vision building and implementation. It is in fact a dynamic and fluid relationship in which the vision of the school is shaped and reshaped as people try to bring about improvements. It is a difficult balance but commitment and skill in the change process on the part of organizational leaders and members is every bit as crucial as ideas about where the school should be heading.

The continuous process of vision building in an organization requires a number of skills and qualities. Two-way communication skills, risk-taking, the balancing of clarity and openness, the combining of pressure and support, integrity, positive regard for others, and a perpetual learning orientation, all figure in the dynamic process of developing a shared vision in the school. In Miles' (1987) terms, the process involves issues of *will* (such as risk taking and tolerance of uncertainty) and *skill* (such as organizational design, the support of others, clear communication, the development of ownership). The shared vision, in short, is about the content of the school as it might become, and the nature of the change process that will get us there.

Consider the result of shared vision building. You and others in the school become the resident experts. You know what you are doing. You know more about the programme than any outsider. You can demonstrate and explain the programme. You are in a better position to deflect unwanted demands because you can point to something substantial. You have critical criteria to serve as a screening mechanism for sorting out which demands to act on seriously and which opportunities to seek. You are, in a word, in a better position to act fearlessly.

8 Decide what you are not going to do

> **The head's job is to ensure that essential things get done, not to do them all himself or herself.**

If the head tries to do everything that is expected, he or she expends incredible energy with little or nothing to show for it. Therefore, one of the most neglected aspects of what's worth fighting for is how to say no and yet maintain, indeed enhance one's reputation and the respect others have for that individual.

There are two features of heads' work which present them with aggravation. One is the endless stream of meetings and new policy and programme directives, already described. The other is a daily schedule which consists of continual interruptions. There are plenty of studies of the individual work days of heads, and they draw the same conclusions: heads' work days are characterized by dozens of small interactions. The research literature has come to label the work of heads as involving brevity, variety, and fragmentation (Peterson, 1985).

Heads, above all, are 'victims of the moment'. Because of the immediacy and physical presence of interruptions, heads are constantly dragged into the crises of the moment. These include telephone calls, two students fighting, salespeople, parents wanting to see them, calls from central office to check into something or to come to an urgent meeting, etc. etc.

Dependency on the moment is not inevitable, however. Four strategies for maintaining initiative and control are: maintaining focus, making your position clear to the superordinates, managing time accordingly and saying no.

Vision building is central to selecting and maintaining focus. To simplify the matter, two issues are of first order

of importance: instructional leadership and public relations. Instructional leadership means working with
teachers and others to decide on the most important needs
of the school, whether it be English as a Second Language,
language and writing across the curriculum, science, or
whatever. Responsiveness to the community is part and
parcel of needs assessment and maintaining focus. Con-
sent, and in some cases involvement of parents, is essential. The priority in relation to the community is
instructionally focused public relations, not random communication.

Making one's position clear to the governors is ideally an
interactive process. The emphasis should be on the head
taking charge. The head, in effect, is saying to the governors that instructional leadership is his or her number one
priority. The particular priorities arrived at may be done in
full cooperation with the governors or in a more distant
manner; in either case, the head makes it a point that the
governors understand the priority and the flow of actions
being taken. The basic message is that if there is an
instructional activity in his or her school and there is a
meeting which conflicts, he or she cannot attend the
meeting but will send someone else. This is not a matter of
being stubborn or rigid. Without such protection, a head's
time would get totally eaten up by unconnected activities
which amount to nothing. By explaining one's position in
terms of specific instructional activities, it turns out that
very few meetings are so important that they cannot be
missed. Many governors would value such a focus and
stance, but let me say some would not. This is where
selective fearlessness comes in. A little assertiveness in
the service of a good cause where you have teacher and
community backing may be necessary. There is nothing
wrong with saying no.

Managing time is related to both attitude and technique.
Protecting priority time, sometimes fiercely, is a must.
Staying focused might mean, for example, setting aside a
morning to plan a professional growth session for staff, and

then sticking to it. It can be made clear that 'nobody is to interrupt' during that time. Exceptions may occur in extreme situations, but telephone calls, even aggressive ones, can be handled by a secretary, delayed or scheduled in.

A second aspect of managing time is how to handle central office events. A head might make a choice not to attend meetings which are purely information. Acting as a filter for unproductive requests is another important component. If the head tries to respond to all central office requests, the school will get pulled in too many different directions. If the meeting is truly important, the head can attend or send someone else who may be more centrally involved with the item being addressed. There is an element of risk taking, but not as much as is assumed when positive instructional focuses are what is driving the head.

Delegation, the third aspect of time management, is an orientation and skill that only a minority of middle managers have mastered. It amounts to the advice to try not to do anything that someone else in the building can do, because heads need to spend their time on what others in the building are not in a position to do. For example, why should a head plan sports days when teachers can do it better because it is for their students? Why should a head collect and count trip money? Why should a head fill out straightforward statistical reports, do the paperwork for teacher absence, and the like? Training secretaries is a related and much undeveloped skill. There is no need for heads to read and answer all the school's mail. There is no need to handle correspondence more than once. Secretaries can be trained to process the mail, answer much of it and bring forward items of significance for action. Secretaries can fill out statistical reports, draft other responses and manage more than they often do. It is not that secretaries have all kinds of time on their hands, but if it is done in conjunction with training on a supportive basis, most secretaries would welcome the autonomy and responsibility because it makes the job more meaningful. Delegation does not mean absence of communication. The head's job is to ensure that essential things get done, not to do them all himself or herself.

Saying 'no' is a summation of the advice of this guideline. Heads spend too much time on things that are not essential. There are few things that absolutely must be done, cannot be delayed or cannot be delegated. Only a small proportion of what heads do is centrally related to instruction apparently. Diversions, of course, also plague heads who have an instructional focus. But, they have learned to say no. Otherwise, the whole day would be spent running around with nothing to show for the effort except stress and with no sense of accomplishment other than short term survival. Heads must get more in the habit of saying no, or rescheduling things for a time when they can be addressed more efficiently. I stress, as I did at the outset, that this is not a matter of letting the head 'off the hook' under the guise of autonomy. The focused, interactive, interdependent head is a socially responsible being, working avidly on the improvement of the school. The effective head is more public than private. Without question, however, what's worth fighting for is saying no to tasks and activities that do not contribute, in a sustained way, to the betterment of the school.

The focused, interactive, interdependent head is a socially responsible being, working avidly on the improvement of the school.

---

9   *Build allies*

It is foolhardy to continue to act fearlessly if you are not at the same time developing alliances. One of the most encouraging developments is the presence of more and more potential allies who seem to want to support and

move in the direction of greater school-based implementation (Fullan *et al.*, 1986). Criteria for promotion tend more
and more to emphasize curricular leadership, capacity for
working effectively with others and ability to lead interactive forms of development whether they involve coaching,
performance appraisal or curriculum implementation.

With this potential, the head should seek alliances,
through specific projects and activities, with at least five
groups – senior level administrators, peers, parents, teachers and individuals who are external to the system (in the
Department of Education, Faculties of Education and so
forth). As Patterson *et al.* note, senior-level administrators
are obviously crucial sources of power as sponsors and as
responders to critical requests (1986: 81).

Peers – other heads and deputy heads – can also be
significant sources of support in the short and long run. It
may require some initiative and risk taking, but heads who
go out of their way to work cooperatively with other heads
on a curriculum project and who share information and
resources, develop both a reputation and a set of relationships which serve them well at points of critical decision.

Alliances with parents are much more tricky. One runs
the risk of getting involved with splinter groups and/or
offending important political forces. Sticking with valued
curriculum priorities can be one safeguard, because work
with the community is intended not to block something,
but to implement something considered to be valuable.

Guideline 6 stressed empowerment of teachers. Such
empowerment is reciprocal. Teachers already have and
exercise power *not* to do things. Building a trusted,
empowered relationship with teachers usually means that
the head can count on teachers to help implement policies
that the head holds to be important.

There are, of course, skills involved in negotiating
relationships across the groups just described. Block (1987)
talks about the critical skills of negotiating agreement and
trust. He complicates the matter, realistically, by noting
that such negotiations must be undertaken with both

allies and adversaries. He outlines a number of steps for dealing with each of the following situations: high agreement/high trust (allies), high trust/low agreement (opponents), high agreement/low trust (bedfellows), low trust/unknown agreement (fence sitters), and low agreement/low trust (adversaries).

This is not the place to delve into these issues. Two conclusions can be made. First, at least *some* allies in each of the five groups should and can be established. In addition to power bases, such a network serves as a source of ideas, critical feedback, and the like. Second, as Block states: 'people become adversaries only when our attempts at negotiating agreement and negotiating trust have failed' (1987: 144).

10   Know when to be cautious

Since people exert so much caution naturally, this section can be brief. Block mentioned four circumstances which dictate caution: when we don't know the situation, when survival is at stake, following periods of risk and expansion, and when we are in a zero trust environment (1987: 17–18). Risks can also be reduced by starting small (and thinking big), trying out ideas on a small scale initially and/or with smaller numbers of people. However, if we are experiencing states of continuous, ever-increasing caution, that is a sign that either we ourselves should change or move elsewhere to a less repressive organization.

> **Err on the side of autonomy over dependency.**

Guidelines for school systems

This booklet is for and about heads, so that the advice for school systems will not be elaborate. Clearly, risk taking in heads will be inhibited if it is not also a characteristic of superordinates. This is so in two ways. Senior level managers who engage in focused risk taking both provide good role models, and create the conditions of pressure and responsiveness for school-level leaders to act similarly.

There are five guidelines which I would highlight:

1 Cherish empowered managers when you find them.
2 Understand the paradoxically simultaneous 'loose-tight' relationship between schools and school systems.
3 Develop system policies and actions which promote 'looseness-tightness'.
4 Concentrate on, and make visible, selection criteria.
5 Establish short- and long-range leadership development plans to produce 'willed and skilled' school leaders.

The first guideline is straightforward – err on the side of autonomy over dependency. Superordinates should value, indeed should cherish, the independent, initiative taking head who has energized the staff and community into working on an instructional issue of importance, even when the superordinate might not fully agree with the particular priority. Empowered heads are not closed-minded, just focused. Openness is maintained through the highly interactive process described in Chapter 2. Put another way, the head's priorities are shaped and reshaped through interaction with teachers, parents, inspectors, governors and LEAs.

Second, understand, conceptualize, and reinforce the paradoxical tight-loose relationships required for modern organizations to be effective. It is not a choice between a 'top-down' system and isolated autonomy. Just as the head must foster autonomy and empowerment of teachers, as outlined in chapter 2, so the central office must do the same in relation to schools. Generally, this means de-centralizing decision-making within a framework of priorities, on the one hand, and staying in close contact throughout the process which involves approving plans, coordinating resources, facilitating networking, reviewing progress and discussing procedures and policies on the other hand.

Louis (1987) captures the essence of the necessarily delicate balancing act in her discussion of loose-tight district management in a study of effective secondary schools. She makes the helpful distinction between coupling and bureaucracy arguing that they are two different dimensions of the relationship:

> By coupling I mean a relationship which has some shared goals and objectives, reasonably clear and frequent communication, and mutual coordination and influence. By bureaucracy I mean control through rules and regulations.
>
> (Louis, 1987: 22)

Drawing on case studies, Louis describes typical and ineffective school districts as evidencing highly bureaucratic but largely decoupled systems. Says Louis, 'in a decoupled but regulatory system the district/school system becomes nothing but an irritating set of constraints and conflicting demands' (p. 24). Strongly coupled regulatory or rule based systems fared no better, and were characterized by mistrust on both sides. By contrast, Louis found that 'the only clearly positive district contexts are found in cases . . . which are *tightly coupled and non-regulatory* . . . Essentially, the picture is one of co-management, with coordination and joint planning . . .' (pp. 25–6, original emphasis). Our own discussion of school level-central level co-development is similar (Fullan *et al.*, 1986). It is imperative then, that superordinates understand that closeness does not mean control, and that autonomy does not mean neglect.

Guideline 3 is a kind of operational version of the policies and actions which will promote non-regulatory closeness, as are guidelines 4 and 5. Curriculum Review, Development and Implementation (CRDI) models, which have school-based decision-making as the corner-stone, represent one strong step. Requiring implementation plans which allow both the goals and strategies to be set at the school level in a system context is one component. Performance appraisal systems which are designed to integrate professional development and curriculum focus, for both teachers and heads, and which stress and reward initiative-taking, is another feature. (See also Duke, 1985, and Hallinger and Murphy, 1985, for suggestions to broaden the criteria for assessing head effectiveness.) Facilitating and coordinating networking across schools and heads is another peer-based strategy which can be powerful in stimulating and supporting action. The idea, in general, is to give the clear message that initiative, active but assessed experimentation and risk taking are expected, and then to have the kinds of procedures and actions which foster, reinforce and reward these behaviours when they occur.

The fourth and fifth guidelines are closely related to each other and to the previous guidelines. The fourth refers to the critical need to establish explicit selection criteria and procedures for promotion, which make it crystal clear that only people who have already demonstrated initiative-taking, curriculum leadership, professional development (interactive forms) leadership, and the like need apply. Nothing conveys the message with greater force, as well as builds a critical mass of mutually stimulating leaders, than decision after decision in which instructionally-oriented and skilled people are promoted.

Short- and long-range leadership development programmes make up the final essential component. The skills and characteristics required of effective school leaders have been discussed at considerable length in Chapter 2. School systems must invest in the mid- and long-range development of potential leaders, and in the continuing professional development of appointed leaders. Internships, short-term secondments and apprenticeships both within the system and external, such as to Faculties of Education or to the DES are important. Mentoring and other structured peer-related approaches would be especially effective. For example, a newly appointed deputy head in one school can work with an experienced head in another school assisting the latter head and teachers in assessing programme implementation, or in designing and carrying out a professional growth programme.

There are a number of other system-based possibilities. Leithwood (1987) describes school system policies for effective school administration. It can be a great help if standard operating policies and procedures systematically stimulate and reinforce interactive autonomy and sustained action. Manasse (1985) and Barth (1986) formulate a number of policy and training steps that should be taken by school systems and by pre and inservice educators. Barnett (1985) describes an effective Peer-Assisted Leadership (PAL) programme in which pairs of heads work with each other in a structured, but non-prescriptive manner in order to analyse and assess their own leadership behaviours, school climate, school programmes and effectiveness.

Pre and on-the-job inservice programmes could also be helpful. Schön's (1987) 'reflective practicum' contains considerable promise for establishing programmes to help school administrators identify situations and to imagine and experiment with actions aimed at increasing autonomy and effectiveness in working with others.

To conclude I would return to the theme of this booklet, which is to beware of system-level approaches for two major reasons. The first is that they externalize the solution and may unwittingly end up fostering further dependency. The second reason is that individual heads cannot afford to wait for school systems to attain this level of achievement. Or, perhaps more accurately, systems will only reach this level through the day-to-day actions of individuals pushing in the other direction.

> **Closeness does not mean control, and autonomy does not mean neglect.**

Perpetual learning

The ultimate safeguard against empowered managers going too far off track is that they are perpetual learners. When it comes to learning, effective leaders are greedy.

Bennis and Nanus (1985) identified a number of common characteristics in their interviews with highly effective leaders. Those interviewed discussed a number of things they do, 'but above all, they talked about learning' (p. 188). Bennis and Nanus continue:

> Nearly all leaders are highly proficient in learning from experience. Most were able to identify a small number of mentors and key experiences that power-fully shaped their philosophies, personalities, and operating style . . . Learning is the essential fuel for the leader, the source of high-octane energy that keeps up the momentum by continually sparking new under-standing, new ideas, and new challenges. It is absol-utely indispensable under today's conditions of rapid change and complexity. Very simply, those who do not learn do not long survive as leaders.
>
> (Bennis and Nanus, 1985: 188)

Kelleher, Finestone and Lowy (1986) provide further insights into 'managerial learning'. In a study of 43 managers, they were able to divide the group into high, medium, and low learners based on an index of seven factors. They found interesting patterns of situations related to high learning – in particular, a combination of freedom, stress, and support. To highlight a few of the factors found in the study, the extent to which the manager was in a situation of expected innovation and latitude, supervisory support and supervisory pressure were cor-related with higher learning. Kelleher and his colleagues also found that high learners experienced more stress.

Block describes the relationship between learning and stress as 'moving toward tension':

> Almost every important learning experience we have

ever had has been stressful. Those issues that create stress for us give us clues about the uncooked seeds within us that need our attention. Stress and anxiety are an indication that we are living our lives and making choices. The entrepreneurial approach is to view tension as a vehicle for discovery. Dissatisfied customers teach us how to do business. People who do not use our services teach us how to sell.

(Block, 1987: 191)

Too much stress is a bad thing, but so is too little. Joy and stress not only can go together, but always coexist in high performers (Hanson, 1985). Turning stress to advantage is very closely related to skill mastery:

The final component of enlightened self-interest is the goal of simply learning as much as you can about the activity that you're engaged in. There's pride and satisfaction in understanding your function better than anyone else and better than even you thought possible. One of the fastest ways to get out of a bureaucratic cycle is to have as your goal to learn as much as you can about what you're doing. Learning and performance are intimately related; the high performers are those who learn most quickly.

(Block, 1987: 86)

The advice for heads, in a nutshell, is to get into the habit of and situations for constant learning. Skill and know-how are as important as attitude. This means access to new ideas and situations, active experimentation, examination of analogous and dissimilar organizations, reflective practice, collegial learning, coaching in relation to practice and more (Schön, 1987). Heads, as perpetual learners, are constantly reaching out for new ideas, seeing what they can learn from others and testing themselves against external standards.

It is not easy to be a perpetual learner under the working conditions faced by heads (Peterson, 1985). Nor is it a matter of random learning from the constant bombardment of demands. Vision-building and other orientations serve as critical screens and extensions to make learning more focused and purposeful. And, if it is any consolation, stressful organizations can present opportunities and conditions more conducive to learning than unstressful ones. Stress, learning, mastery, and impact are closely interconnected.

Organizations do not get healthy by themselves, and we all would be extremely lucky if our organization got healthy through someone else's efforts other than our own. Managing in a nonrational world means counting on our own selves:

> This is the true joy in life, the being used for a purpose recognized by yourself as a mighty one; the being a force of nature instead of a feverish selfish little clod of ailments and grievances complaining that the world will not devote itself to making you happy. I want to be thoroughly used up when I die, for the harder I work the more I live. I rejoice in life for its own sake. Life is no 'brief candle' to me. It is a sort of splendid torch which I have got hold of for the moment, and I want to make it burn as brightly as possible before handing it on to future generations.
> (From Shaw's *Man and Superman* quoted in Bennis and Nanus, 1985: 32)

Paradoxically, counting on oneself for a good cause in a highly interactive organization is the key to fundamental *organizational change*. People change organizations. The starting point is not system change, or change in those around us, but taking action ourselves. The challenge is to improve education in the only way it can be – through the day-to-day actions of empowered individuals. This is what's worth fighting for in school headship.

> **The challenge is to improve education in the only way it can be – through the day-to-day actions of empowered individuals.**

REFERENCES

Barnett, B. (1985). ' A synthesis for improving practice'. Paper presented at the annual meeting of the American Education Research Association.

Barth, R. (1986). 'The principal and the profession of teaching', *The Elementary School Journal*, **86**: 471–92.

Bennis, W. and Nanus, B. (1985). *Leaders*. New York: Harper & Row.

Block, P. (1987). *The Empowered Manager*. San Francisco: Jossey-Bass.

Bossert, S., Dwyer, D., Rowan, B. and Lee, G. (1982). 'The instructional management role of the principal', *Educational Administration Quarterly*, **18**: 34–64.

Cox, P., French, L. and Loucks-Horsley, S. (1987). 'Getting the principal off the hotseat: configuring leadership and support for school improvement', Andover, Mass.: The Regional Laboratory for Educational Improvement.

Drucker, P. (1985). *Innovation and Entrepreneurship*. New York: Harper & Row.

Duke, D. (1985). 'Should principals be required to be effective', *School Organization*, **5**: 125–46.

Edu-Con (1984). *The Role of the Public School Principal in the Toronto Board of Education.* Toronto: Educ-Con of Canada.

Fullan, M. (1992). *Successful School Improvement.* Buckingham: Open University Press.

Fullan, M. with Stiegelbauer, S. (1991). *The Meaning of Educational Change.* 2nd edition, London: Cassell.

Fullan, M. and Hargreaves, A. (1992). *What's Worth Fighting For in Your School?* Buckingham: Open University Press.

Fullan, M., Anderson, S. and Newton, E. (1986). *Support Systems for Implementing Curriculum in School Boards.* Toronto: OISE Press, and Ontario Government Bookstore.

Fullan, M. and Connelly, M. with Watson, N. (1987). *Teacher Education in Ontario: Current Practice and Options for the Future.* Final position paper prepared for the Ontario Ministry of Colleges and Universities and Ministry of Education.

Fullan, M., Park, P., Williams, T., Allison, P., Walker, L. and Watson, N. (1987). *Supervisory Officers in Ontario: Current Practice and Recommendations for the Future.* Final Report to the Ontario Ministry of Education.

Fullan, M., Miles, M. and Anderson, S. (1988). 'Strategies for implementing micro-computers: The Ontario Case'. Ontario Ministry of Education.

Hall, G. (1987). 'The principal as leader of the change facilitating team'. Paper presented at the annual meeting of the American Education Research Association.

Hall, G., Hord, S. and Griffin, T. (1980). 'Implementation at the school building level'. Austin: R&D Center for Teacher Education.

Hallinger, P. and Murphy, J. (1985). 'Assessing the instructional leadership behavior of principals', *The Elementary School Journal*, **86**: 217–48.

Hanson, P. (1985). *The Joy of Stress.* Toronto: Hanson Stress Management Organization.

Hord, S. and Hall, G. (1987). 'Three images: what principals do in curriculum implementation', *Curriculum Inquiry*, **17**: 55–89.

Inner London Education Authority (1985). *The Junior School Project.* London, England: ILEA.

Kelleher, D., Finestone, P. and Lowy, A. (1986). 'Managerial learning: first notes from an unstudied frontier', *Group & Organization Studies*, **VII**: 169–202.

Leavitt, H. (1986). *Corporate Pathfinders*. Homewood, Illinois: Dow Jones-Irwin.

Leithwood, K. and Montgomery, D. (1982). 'The role of the elementary school principal in program improvement', *Review of Educational Research*, **52**: 309–39.

Leithwood, K. and Montgomery, D. (1986). *The Principal Profile*. Toronto: OISE Press.

Leithwood, K. (1987). 'School system policies for effective school administration'. Unpublished paper, OISE.

Lortie, D. (1987). 'Built-in tendencies toward stabilizing the principal's role'. Paper presented at the annual meeting of the American Education Research Association.

Louis, K. (1987). 'The role of school districts in school innovation'. Paper prepared for conference on Organizational Policy for School Improvement. Toronto: OISE.

Manasse, L. (1985). 'Improving conditions for principal effectiveness', *The Elementary School Journal*, **85**: 439–63.

Miles, M. (1987). 'Practical guidelines for school administrators: how to get there'. Paper presented at the annual meeting of the American Education Research Association.

Mortimore, P., Sammons, P., Stoll, L. *et al.* (1988). *School Matters: The Junior Years*. Somerset: Open Books.

Ottawa Board of Education. (1984). 'Committee on overloading the elementary curriculum'. Ottawa Board of Education.

Patterson, J., Purkey, S. and Parker, J. (1986). *Productive School Systems for a Nonrational World*. Alexandria, Virginia: Association for Supervision and Curriculum Development.

Peters, T. (1987) *Thriving on Chaos: Handbook for a Management Revolution*. New York: A. Knopf.

Peters, T. and Waterman, R. (1982). *In Search of Excellence*. New York: Harper & Row.

Peterson, K. (1985). 'Obstacles to learning from experience and principal training', *The Urban Review*, **17**: 189–200.

Sarason, S. (1982). *The Culture of the School and the Problem of Change*. 2nd edition, Boston: Allyn & Bacon.

Schön, D. (1987). *Educating the Reflective Practitioner.* San Francisco: Jossey-Bass.

Trider, D. and Leithwood, K. (1988). 'Influences on principal's practices', *Curriculum Inquiry*, **18**(3): 289–311.